"This book is about so much more than death, divorce, or separation; it's about life. Whether or not you've gone through any of these things, Isaiah's words will strike a chord with you. Rarely does an author attack a subject—much less his own life—with such brutal honesty."

DR. TOM HILL, co-author of *Chicken Soup for the Entrepreneur's Soul* and author of *Living at the Summit*

"Isaiah Stratton leads us through his own darkness and into the God-given light of hope."

DOUG JONES, star of Pan's Labyrinth, Hellboy 1 & 2, and F4: Rise of the Silver Surfer

---

"I laughed. I cried. But most importantly—I contemplated. I was completely unprepared for the journey Isaiah took me on. At times, I had to put the book down just to sit silently and experience the emotion it stirred. 'Suddenly Single' paves the way from brokenness to beauty. . .and it is a road well worth taking."

TORRY MARTIN, award-winning actor, screenwriter and author who created the popular character of 'Wooton Bassett' for Focus on the Family's audio drama "Adventures in Odyssey"

Printed in the U.S.A.

© 2014 Isaiah Stratton
All rights reserved

ISBN 978-0-9916092-0-8 (trade paper)
ISBN 978-0-9916092-1-5 (eBook)

All the events in this book are true. Some of the sequences have been rearranged, and, in certain cases, the names and identifying details of individuals have been changed.

Cover photography: Katie Butler *katiebutlerstudios.com*
Cover design and interior layout: Amy Lyon

isaiahstratton.com

ISAIAH STRATTON
SUDDENLY**SINGLE**

CONTENTS

1	Abandoned	11
2	Weddings	17
3	Lawyers	25
4	Christmas	31
5	New Year's	37
6	Deployment	43
7	Summer	47
8	Protect	53
9	Death	59
10	Divorce	69
11	Down	75
12	Turn	81
13	Live	89
	Afterword	99
	Notes	101

ACKNOWLEDGMENTS

CONTRIBUTORS TO THIS BOOK:
Cecil "Cec" Murphey, who generously mentored me, believed in my story, and pushed me to hone my craft. Rebecca English, my editor who took my words and polished them tirelessly. Dusten Carlson and Michelle Grover, who took the time to read my early drafts and gave me wonderful feedback. Katie Butler, Josh Lyon, and Amy Lyon, whose artistry helped turn this story into reality.

MY SOUNDING BOARDS:
Uncle Dicky and Aunt Holly, Abe and Liz, Cory and Jennifer—thanks for the talks, the texts, and for listening when I needed to vent.

THE INCREDIBLE CROWD-FUNDING FANS:
When I launched my campaign to raise the funds for the publication of this book, I never dreamed I would reach my goal in less than twenty-four hours. Thanks to all who contributed and especially to the incredible generosity of the following:

Shannon Beck, Colter Bergh, Steven and Laura Brundage, Stephen Cleary, Chris Davis, Kurt Day, Chris Domke, Adam Ferguson, Justin and Sarah Fox, Camilo Franco, Dr. Joe Gibson, Chris Hamblen, Drew Hamblen, Elijah Hamblen, Steve and Cindy Hamblen, Pete and Shelley Hansen, Melissa Holloway, Johnroy Joseph, Matthew King, Anne Laiho, James A Lee, Randy and Pat Lee, Richard Lupp, Page Lynch, Nicholas Mastropietro, Nick and Rosie Mastropietro, Ron Milne, Craig and Kim O'Rourke, Hannah Paxton, Marti Pletcher, Cory and Jennifer Rexford,

Matthew "Colonel" Ridenhour, Olan Rogers, Dennis Rozak, Jason Russell, Heath Satterfield, Dan and Jean Shumaker, Kevin Sievers, Byron and Allison Smith, Steven Stadtmiller, Chelsea Steen, Abe and Liz Stratton, Cory Vetter, and Julie Zimmer.

HONORABLE MENTIONS:

Starbucks, Frothy Monkey, and Fido, places where I spent hours letting the coffee nudge the words from my brain onto my keyboard. "The Mighty Rio Grande" by This Will Destroy You—I don't know how many hundreds of times I played this song while writing. At some point it became the unofficial soundtrack for this book.

To my family who has always loved me, thank you.

To the One who has never left me, I pray that these broken words somehow give voice to the gratitude I hold for You.

for the broken ones

1

ABANDONED

The sensation is absolutely nonverbal, but everybody knows it even without words: the stunned breathlessness that follows a jab to the solar plexus. What will astonish me in the days to come is that this sensation can sustain itself long after one would expect to be dead of asphyxiation. I have often wished myself dead. If it were possible to die of grief, I would die at this moment. But it's not, and I don't.

Nancy Mairs, Ordinary Time

I was alone.

I sipped my coffee, not even tasting it. She was gone, and that was all that mattered. Nothing in life had prepared me for this moment. School, military, work: all tools that had shaped the shell of the man I now was. None of those tools helped me when my heart was ripped out.

Turning, I stared at the room—a room that had once been so significant to both of us. Beside the sink, a framed collage filled the spot next to the drying rack. Smiling faces grinned at me. Picking up the frame, I slid into a chair at the table. Two ghosts from my past beckoned, dancing within their two-dimensional prisons. We laughed about the inside jokes from our summer hiking trip. We glowed in the setting sun overlooking Cincinnati, the brilliant diamond flashing on her finger. We basked in the sparkling white sands of the Mexican resort, faces radiating the passions of the newly married. We posed in dress blues and scarlet cocktail gown before dashing off to the Marine Corps Ball.

I made no attempt to stop the rushing tears. If there had just been some way to rewind time, I would have paid any price to do it.

I sat until it was so dark that I couldn't see the dregs in the bottom of my cup. Pushing the mug away, I stood up, gently replaced the frame, let myself out the back door, and stepped from under the awning into the cold rain. The South Carolina downpour saturated my shirt as I crossed to the mailbox. My hand mechanically opened it the same way it had done hundreds of times before.

Empty.

Pivoting in the wet grass, my gaze roamed over our little house. Empty front windows stared at me. Flowers I'd planted months earlier bowed wearily in their beds. Moldering mulch eroded around them and bled into the yard. The rain pounded a dirge on the angled roof.

I wiped the water from my eyes as I stepped back into the kitchen. A whispering sound approached from the hall.

"What are you doing, Trooper?"

The sound of my own voice jarred me as I broke the silence. She coiled her way around my ankles, back and forth, back and forth, waiting for me to pet her.

Reaching down, I realized that she was gone. A rumbling meow came from the corner by the food dish.

"All right, all right, I'm coming."

Scooping up the feed bowl, I bent to fill it and stepped splat in the middle of a puddle.

"Stupid cat!"

She had an insidious habit of batting the water out of her bowl onto the kitchen floor—the gurgle of the bubbles in the water reservoir intrigued her.

My right sock was soaked. I aimed the plastic feed bowl at the corner where I'd last heard her, but she had anticipated me and streaked into the living room where I could hear her scurrying under the sofa. This wasn't her first rodeo.

Flicking on the kitchen light, I stuck my head into the living room. Two green mirrors addressed me from the darkness under the couch.

"I'm sorry. I wasn't mad at you. She's gone, and I don't know what to do. It doesn't look like she's coming back. She said she'll pick you up in a few days, so let's just keep the peace, okay?"

She slunk back to her bowl, stuck her paw in the water, and looked at me.

"You're not helping things."

She innocently rubbed her paw over her head, cleaning herself.

"Come here." I scooped her up, and it was one of those rare moments when she went still. I scratched her under the chin in her favorite spot. Her eyes closed, and the throbbing rumble in her throat went into high gear.

"I'm actually going to miss you. Who am I supposed to talk to once you're gone too?"

I wandered into the dark living room and sank into my favorite chair, looking across the room at the empty couch. A lightning bolt popped, illuminating the spot where *she* always sat designing her latest artwork. The whole room felt off balance without her. The emptiness of the house breathed in my ears. I couldn't take it much longer.

We walked across the deserted theater parking lot, bracing ourselves against the chill of the winter night. As we neared the car, she rested her head on my shoulder, entwining both her arms through mine and pulling me close. Through my coat I felt the warmth of her body pressed against my side. Tracing my thumb along her cheekbone, I brushed a rebellious lock of raven hair behind her ear.

The dream always ended the same: the upturned face, the luminous brown eyes, and the way her lips moved as she cupped my face and whispered, "I'm so happy."

I jerked awake, my pillow sticky with sweat. The dreams were infrequent, but when they came, they were with such lucidity that it took me several minutes to pull myself back into reality. I lay on the left side of the bed—my side. When we had first moved into the house, I had taken the side closest to the door—part of my protective instinct. My right arm now reached over to the emptiness beside me. I wanted her body—nothing sexual, just the person, the companionship. I clamped my eyes shut, praying for sleep.

Minutes passed with the whoosh of the ceiling fan filling the ticking seconds. It felt so natural to talk to Him. Where had that familiarity been for the past months? Months? Wait, who was I kidding? It had been years.

The memories are part of who you are now. I had to get your attention.

"You could have gotten my attention another way. I'm not that stupid!" Rubbing my knuckles into gritty eyes, I sat up trembling. "You think tearing my heart apart, taking the one person who means the world to me, was the only way?"

The pain was ripping at me again. My hands shook, and my breath came in ragged gasps. The memory of our last kiss sliced through my mind. We had been standing in the corner of the bedroom eight feet from where I now lay. As our lips parted, I felt something else separate too.

"Isaiah, I'm leaving."

I stared at her, unable to process what she was saying.

"But baby, please. I love you—" I choked up, unable to get the words out.

Tears brimmed in her eyes, but she shook her head. "It's no use…"

I watched her lips moving, but I couldn't hear the words. The room seemed like it was tilting. She was my first love, my only love, and she was leaving.

"Please, please, don't. Just give us one more chance—"

She shook her head, and two tears broke loose and coursed down her face. "It's no use. I can't do this anymore." She looked so small, so frightened, and yet so different. Despite the tears, her body was stiff as if she were determined not to break down. Her eyes were cold.

I reached out for her as I'd done thousands of times. This time she pulled back. A different woman looked up at me. "I don't want to hurt you—"

"Not hurt me? *Not hurt me?* You're killing me. I've built my life around you and now—"

"Don't." She held up her hand. The voice that followed was hard, foreign. "There's nothing else to say. I'm leaving."

My mind seemed like a dislocated joint, sensing circumstances but unable to respond to them, and in that moment, I saw the end.

Divorce—that horrible nightmare—was happening.

It was happening to us. And there was nothing I could do about it. Me: the guy trained to kill, to adapt, and to protect. I was a warrior machine undone by the only enemy capable of defeating me—my own apathy. Years earlier I had fought for and captured her heart. But over the past several months, I had rarely stepped onto the battlefield. Now it was too late. She had trusted my hands to hold her, and I had let her slip away.

Now His voice spoke again. *You spent so many years convinced that you could handle it all. Will you listen to Me now?*

I could only nod. I rolled over, pulling her pillow to me, holding it desperately.

The months and years ahead will be the most painful you've ever experienced, but I promise you that I have a plan. Will you trust Me?

I was a wounded animal, cornered, ready to bite the first helping hand extended to it.

I didn't want to trust. I just wanted to give up.

2

WEDDINGS

Hope.

The word mocked me.

I picked up the small, smooth stone and rubbed it between my fingers, feeling the cold, even texture broken only by the tiny letters carved into it.

"We're so glad you could all be here at our rehearsal dinner." Byron reached down and squeezed Allison's hand. She smiled up at him.

"The stones on the tables in front of you have different character traits etched into them. Allison and I are asking that you each take one and use it as a reminder to keep us and our marriage in your prayers."

I sat at a table with several people I had never met. There hadn't been any question about whether or not I would come to the wedding. Byron and Allison were great friends, and I had agreed to help with some of the set up and tear down responsibilities for the dinner.

Leaning back, I ignored the undercurrent of conversation, my attention caught by the little stream of stones running down the center of the tables: *Love, Joy, Hope, Peace.*

I rubbed my stone methodically. Of course I would pray for my friends' marriage. And I would keep praying for mine. The weight of the rock gave me a small feeling of peace that there was still certainty in the world. Maybe it wasn't too late for a miracle. Maybe there still was hope.

Maybe.

Sliding into my truck after the dinner, I felt the rock in my pocket pressing into my thigh. I took it out and absentmindedly turned it in my hand as I drove. Over and over I ran my thumb over the letters, praying that somewhere some glimmer of hope would come back into my life.

Who was I kidding? Hope? A little rock? What was I thinking? Nothing was going to change.

I opened my glove compartment, threw the rock inside, and slammed it shut.

I was early.

I sat in the parking lot of the reception venue watching vehicles fill up the rows in front of the rustic building. The reception tent was visible in the rear of the property. Flower-covered walkways guided the guests to the tent's entrance. I nervously drummed my fingers on the armrest, stopping when I saw her car pull in. The driver's side door opened, and a man's leg swung out. My stomach knotted, and my hand unconsciously went for my door handle until I realized that her dad had driven her car to the reception.

I sat back, forcing myself to relax. For the past month since she had left, I had dreaded this wedding. Few things are more awkward than attending a wedding at which your estranged wife will be present. What made it even more painful was that her younger sister, Kate, was getting married. Kate had lived with us for a year, and during that time she had become as close to me as my own siblings.

We had spent years watching Kate's dating life, celebrating with her during the ups and encouraging her during the downs. When Brannon—a college friend from years before—had come back into her life, we had excitedly watched as their relationship blossomed. I guess you could have called it a whirlwind romance, because they had gone from dating to engagement to wedding in less than a year. Their wedding was supposed to be a huge celebration, and it was—for everyone except me. I felt not only the loss of her but the loss of her family as well.

I wiped my sweating hands on my pants and forced my breathing to slow. I wasn't going to show pain, not today. I didn't care what kind of confused looks I'd get when I walked in alone. No one deserved an answer today. I steeled myself against the pain of seeing her family. The pain of seeing her.

I swallowed the excuses. Delaying the inevitable wouldn't help. It was Kate and Brannon's day. Stepping from my truck, I headed for the tent. It was hard not to notice all the couples—people in twos everywhere I looked.

Soft lights rimmed the roof while the evening breeze gently pushed through the open sides. Big-band music swelled while people hovered around the reception tables like so many bumblebees. Standing in line waiting for a drink, I was glad I didn't know the people in front of and behind me; they must have been co-workers of Kate's. I poured my drink slowly—anything to spare myself from the moment when I'd turn and see some familiar, pitying face.

A beautiful arrangement of flowers positioned on a pedestal adjacent to the drink table attracted my attention, offering my best option for hiding in plain sight.

Across the room I saw her talking to her family. She was impossible to miss with her strapless gray dress, beautiful shoulders, cascading raven hair. How could I still be so attracted to her? My stomach twisted, and I slipped out of the tent and headed for the men's restroom attached to the rear of the building. I made sure that I was alone before bolting the door behind me. Leaning both hands on the sink, I shook my head, trying to clear it of the memories of my own wedding day—so simple and beautiful but now so long ago.

Dull eyes stared back at me in the mirror. I wanted to find Kate and Brannon, grab them, plead with them to understand what this day meant—what it *really* meant. The garbage the media spouted was lies: our lover won't always be there for us; we won't always feel the infatuation we feel at the beginning.

The beautiful thing they were beginning was at once the most amazing and most difficult thing they would ever face.

Why had it taken me so long to realize that?

Why hadn't I started fighting until it was too late?

I slammed the block wall with my fist.

Drops of sweat glistened on my forehead while a muscle tremor worked its way down my neck. A dead, thousand-yard stare that I hadn't seen since boot camp glared at me from the mirror. A splash of cold water washed the heat from my face and jarred me back to the present. I mashed a handful of paper towels against my knuckles until the bleeding stopped, and then I headed back to the tent.

A half hour later, I snagged the bride and groom. They were making the rounds of well-wishers, showering hugs and smiles on friends and family, accepting loving congratulations and kisses. Kate looked as if she'd just stepped off the pages of a *Free People* catalog in her gypsy-inspired dress, the gap between her top teeth appearing every time she flashed her radiating smile. Brannon, dapper as ever in a pair of linen trousers and suspenders, stood beside her looking, if possible, even more excited than she did.

"Istra!" she yelped and grabbed me in a hug. Years earlier, we'd labeled each other with nicknames that still stuck. In college, where we'd met, full student IDs had consisted of the first initial and the beginning of the last name followed by the student's ID number. Kate had opted to drop the numbers on mine and to stick me with the remaining handle.

I laughed as I spun her around. "You look amazing, Emo. Your dress—I've got no words. Hard to believe the big day has finally come. I'm so glad I could be here to see it."

"And well done to you, *sir*," I added, grabbing Brannon's hand. A fellow Marine, I had always enjoyed any chance to give him grief about his officer status. "Still not sure how you got so lucky."

He kissed the top of Kate's head. "Me neither."

Kate smiled up at him, sliding her hand into his, her intricately designed ring glowing in the low light.

Brannon grabbed me in a hug. "We're glad you came. It means so much to Kate and me."

There was that extra split-second squeeze, the one that says exactly what words cannot. Beside his, Kate's face took on a subdued tone. Pain flashed behind her hazel eyes. I caught her sideways glance across the room.

"Istra, I'm so—"

"Stop." I didn't mean for it to sound as harsh as it did.

They were a picture of love, of ecstasy. That day—a celebration of union—I wanted her with me so badly. I wanted an arm around mine, the familiar, beautiful form warm by my side, the buffer that had always made the intimidating realm of social interaction easier to face. My fingers were cold. I shoved them into my pockets.

"This night is a treasure, and you'll always remember it," I said. "Bottle it up, and enjoy returning to it in the years ahead."

I looked at Brannon, my voice softening. "I know your deployment is coming. A year's a long time." At this, Emo tucked in closer to him, tightening her grip. His ship date to Afghanistan was only months away. "I wish there were some way that I could trade places with you, man."

"Thanks," he replied. "I know you mean that."

We stood silent for a second, sharing the bond of military brotherhood, before I squeezed Kate one final time. "Take these next few months, and live a lifetime together. Don't let the little things rock you. You guys are going to be okay. I love you. Now go." They looked like a dream as they floated away.

My focus swung to the far corner of the room where she stood. My throat constricted, acid burned my eyes, and my jaw muscles clenched involuntarily. How was it possible to hurt this much?

I had to get out. I slipped from the tent and made my way to the parking lot. The quiet safety of my truck broke my reserve; salt washed away biting acid. I don't remember how long I sat shaking, gripping the wheel, and praying for a reprieve from the pain.

"Where are You in all this?"

I punched the steering wheel and swore as the gash on my hand split open. Reaching across to the empty passenger seat, I touched it, trying to remember when it used to be warm. Blood oozed from my battered knuckles, and my eyes moved to the scar on the back of my hand.

My mind wandered, and I could feel her fingers interlaced with mine. Years earlier when we had first been dating, she had slipped her hand into mine while I drove. She had gently traced the scar and asked what had happened. I had been on a training exercise in the California desert, and a piece of flaming nylon had landed on my hand, leaving a deep burn. It was those little moments I missed—how observant she was, how she noticed the small things, how she noticed me.

I'm working on you, and it's going to hurt. I know you're angry. Run to Me, child. Give Me the chance to show you the plans I have for you. I'm not here to hurt you but to give you hope. Be still now and know Me.

Driving away, I glanced back at twinkling lights morphing into blurred orbs through the tears.

3

LAWYERS

"A small dusty man in a small dusty room." The opening line from the Alistair MacLean novel I'd read two decades earlier echoed in my ears as I stepped into the lawyer's office: a small, windowless space cluttered with filing cabinets, chairs, and the kind of pointless wall paintings you'd find at any cheap decoration shop, the air redolent with the aroma of musky papers and leather-bound law books. Peering up from behind his computer, he motioned me to a chair—the only one not occupied with teetering towers of legal pads.

"Isaiah?"

"Yes. Thanks for seeing me."

"I'm Jonathan. My secretary said that you had some paperwork you wanted me to look over?"

The paperwork had appeared in my mailbox as late fall collapsed into a dismal winter. Pulling out the manila envelope in the evening chill, I had felt a lead weight drop from my heart through the pit of my stomach.

"That's right. It's all very straightforward, but I just wanted someone else to check it for me to make sure I wasn't missing anything."

He nodded sagely, looking for all the world like a stockbroker noting the latest index. His eyes flickered to the corner of the desk where the papers lay. "I see. And this is the agreement?"

"Yes."

I hunkered down in the chair, pulling my coat around me while he perused the document. At one point he asked for clarification on a matter pertaining to the house. Laying the papers down, he surveyed the dismal landscape of the room, muttering something about an additional form. Opening a creaking cabinet behind him, he shuffled through reams of paper. I could almost hear the tiny cries of the divorced souls of the past floating out from the dark hole. How many others were in there?

"Bear with me one moment while I call Craig's office to clarify this one issue." He pressed the speaker button, allowing me to follow along.

I nodded. I wasn't going anywhere.

Craig picked up on the second ring, his disembodied voice crawling out of the speaker. He and Jonathan had obviously spoken before.

"Craig, Jonathan here. I've got Mr. Stratton in my office, and I'm reviewing the separation agreement your office sent to him. There's one clarification needed on the sale of the house. Now if we…"

Mind-numbing disbelief seeped into me. I sat listening to these two men discussing the termination of a marriage, the severing of two lives, the shredding of shared dreams, like two flea-market-booth operators discussing the weather—

absence of emotion, cryptic notes, and legalese—two wooden tennis players batting a tired ball back and forth. I wondered if this was how they dealt with watching marriages die day in and day out: remove the human element—look at it as business and nothing else.

I could understand the concept. It was the same way they had trained us to kill. Dehumanize the target, disassociate any personal element, repeat the motions until they become nothing more than muscle memory: the arm reacting, involuntarily shooting, fingers aiming for eye sockets, maiming, disabling—easing the final aim of "target neutralized." No thought precedes the double heel strike to the face, the driving of the boot into the head, the shattering of the skull.

If your enemy's not human, then real killing means nothing more than a butt stock to the face and a bayonet in the hard plastic abdomen of another tattered dummy. Was this how these lawyers did it? It was the only thing that made sense to me.

"That about wraps it up, Craig. Hey, are you going to that business brunch next week?"

The metallic voice crackled in response.

"I'm not sure yet either. Okay, well, adjust the wording on that one paragraph, and send it out again."

He thumbed the speaker key and looked up at me. I struggled to reconnect the humanity to the situation. Leaning forward in his overstuffed chair, he capped his fountain pen.

"His office will mail out the revised agreement in a few days. Did you have any further questions for me?"

His abrupt query caught me off guard. I had a million questions but only one more he could answer. I shifted in my seat. "Is there nothing else I can do?"

"Uh, I'm not sure I follow."

"I mean, this is it? Some papers get filed, a year later my marriage is over, and there's nothing I can do about it?"

Two fish eyes bulged back at me from behind thick glasses perched on a squashed nose, empty of answers, empty of anything useful to me.

"Uh, no, Mr. Stratton, there… there's not. Once the papers are filed, the only thing you can do is to draw out the process. The end result is inevitable, I'm afraid."

I felt like a skydiver who's been handed a pack full of bricks and told to enjoy his jump. Standing, I muttered, "Well, thank you for your time."

He stood, reached out a small soft hand, and shook mine. "Best of luck."

The retort that came to my mind would have gotten me thrown out of most places. I settled for a terse nod and left him there. A small dusty man in a small dusty room.

The fading winter sun threw a watery glare through the window as I let myself in. The house sat completely still; even the blustering wind outside had died. I flicked on my stereo. Mechanically, I unclasped my watch and pulled open my top drawer to drop the timepiece in. My eyes rested on my .40 caliber pistol tucked into the drawer's back corner, and for a second I just stared at it.

Wrapping my hand around the familiar grip, I turned it in my hand, feeling the cold reassurance of the molded metal—a tool I understood, something that didn't ask unanswerable questions, that provided a solution for problems. Ejecting the magazine, I looked at the row of neatly stacked hollow point rounds. With the unthinking habit of practiced repetition, I slammed the mag home, yanked the slide back, and heard the oiled mechanism chamber the round. I brought my hands up, the pistol simply an extension of my arms, and gazed over the white dot sights, watching everything blur away except that one steady front post.

How many hundreds, thousands, of times had I done this? It was so easy. Turning the pistol, I looked down the yawning barrel. The ingenuity of it all still fascinated me: death, just inches away.

And why not? Nothing mattered. Two lawyers in offices miles away were orchestrating the destruction of the world as I knew it. I was powerless, a strong man fighting the wind. No one would care.

I flipped the safety catch and put the muzzle against my chest, just to the side of the sternum. I'd at least give my family an open casket. The hollow point would mushroom through my heart—I saw morbid images of a sledge hammer caving my chest, blood and bone fragments splattering the wall, acrid powder burning my nose, light receding. I played with the trigger, knowing the exact pressure that would engage the firing pin.

I have plans for you.

I cursed, squeezing the trigger more tightly.

Listen, child.

"I want out! Do You hear me? I want out! I'm just a dead man walking."

The blood pounding in my ears almost deafened me. I'd never been this close before. The emptiness was sucking the life from me. My core unconsciously tightened, anticipating the impact.

Listen.

I could hear the music from the stereo suddenly, clearly filling my mind, Fee's "Arms that Hold the Universe" calling out to me.

He whispered to me through the words, reassuring my wrecked heart.

I slid down the wall, chest heaving. Wrapping my arms around my legs I rocked back and forth, howling till my vocal chords went ragged.

Rest, child. I promise that I will you hold you tonight. She left you, but I promise that I never will. When your nights seem darkest, that is when I will be closest to you.

I don't even remember getting off the floor or climbing into bed. The next thing I remember was sunlight filtering through the curtains, waking me after a night of dreamless sleep, the pistol still gripped in my hand.

4

CHRISTMAS

I navigated my truck between the vehicles parked outside my uncle and aunt's house as the street lamps feebly greeted the evening twilight. Shoving the gear shift into park, I looked up at the house. Christmas lights rimmed the windows. Inside I could see blurred figures rushing about.

The raw hole inside me had slowly filled with ice over the past few weeks. I moved from hyper emotion to the complete opposite end of the spectrum. Christmas—the one holiday when you want those closest to you, well, closest to you. And here I was alone.

My hands still rested on the wheel, and I glanced at my watch—the Guess watch she had bought for me two Christmases earlier, the kind with interchangeable bands, one metal and one leather. I always left it on the leather cuff; it just felt right.

Memories. Memories everywhere I turned. I forced a smile. No sense in ruining everyone else's night. Grabbing the presents off the passenger seat, I took a deep breath and headed for the front door.

Several hours later, Christmas dinner dispatched, presents opened, hugs exchanged, the elephant in the room having been tactfully ignored, I began to itch to leave. Sometimes I wanted to be around people, but the minute I was, I wanted to be alone again. After so much solitude, even a couple voices started feeling deafening. Using the excuse of checking my phone, I stepped into a side room for a moment of quiet. A couple voices outside the door caught my attention.

"Isn't it just so sad?"

"I know. His grandfather would be rolling over in his grave if he saw this."

I didn't hear anymore. The ice inside me spread to my extremities. I felt completely alone, castigated, a mar on this family that, so far, had been blessed to avoid divorce.

Grandpa had been a big bear of a man who had died unexpectedly as he had taken a break between pickup basketball games. I had never really had the chance to get to know him, since he had passed when I was barely a teenager, but I had always loved his gentle stoicism and quiet kindness.

I felt like a failure all over again. Was this what my family thought of me—that I was someone who had brought shame on the impeccable family name? I'd experienced rejection by the person who meant the most to me. If anyone else wanted to join the bandwagon of criticism at this point, well, that was fine. I was too numb to care.

Quietly, I made my rounds of saying goodbye and slipped out into the night. I had to run, to clear my head, to escape. The moment I got back to the house, I grabbed a hoodie, threw on my running shoes, and hit the road. The inky blackness overhead yawned in a glittering expanse, the crystalline air icy on my face as I turned onto the main strip, the road a desolate gash in the night landscape. Here was my solace, my retreat. The road was always there for me, never judging me, never caring what I wore, what I was listening to, what kind of day I'd had; it simply welcomed me.

My mom liked to say that I marched to the beat of a different drum. I had joined the Marines straight out of high school, enlisting when no one else in my family ever had. My grandpa on my mom's side had been drafted in the Korean War, but as far as I knew, I was the only one ever to volunteer. Why had I always felt so different, even out of place at times?

I still remembered the jokes, the laughs when my buddies found out I was still a virgin.

"Dude, you've never slept with a girl? What are you waiting for?"

"Waiting till I get married."

"So you've never—"

"Nope."

"Not even—"

"No."

"What?"

A wry smile cracked my face as I remembered the good-natured ribbings. Transitioning from an uber-conservative background straight into the Marine Corps wasn't exactly normal. I learned more about sex in my first week of boot camp then I'd learned in my entire life up to that point. But it was after basic, at my Military Occupational Specialty schooling at Redstone Arsenal, that I really had the chance to live out my beliefs. There was no accountability there. I had the opportunities to do whatever I wanted, but I saved myself, and it was then that I really realized how closely my buddies watched me.

The respect came gradually, but over the years the relationships I built with those guys opened the doors for me to be Christ to foul-mouthed jarheads who would never darken a church doorstep. They could smell hypocrisy a mile away. But once you took your stand and stuck to it, you earned the respect.

But that had been a lifetime ago. After eight years, I had taken my honorable discharge. Now I felt incredibly alone. I actually missed my rough brothers and the camaraderie we'd had. With them I had been the straight-laced Christian, the guy who didn't get drunk, the one who always got everyone back to the barracks in one piece, the good guy. But with my family I felt like a black sheep.

Checking my watch, I made the turn at the four-mile point; I just didn't feel like making it a full ten tonight. Circling, I encountered a blasting headwind. At times like these I relished thrashing my body. It gave me an outlet for my pain, exchanging the sodden throb of the ice in my heart for the tearing scream of stretched lungs and tired legs. I let my mind glide into neutral as the miles passed, and I began to accept the reality of what was before me. A life bereft of a partner, a gaping hole that God had allowed, forcing my focus back to Him.

It was too early for sleep. I found myself aimlessly straightening closets, trying to maintain some order in the chaos. Something caught my eye in the darkness of the high shelf, a shoebox half-covered with shopping bags. I pried it loose, swiping the dust away. Lifting the lid free, I choked. My vision swam as I stood there shaking. I reached behind me for a chair. The tight, familiar script of my own handwriting looked up at me—the box of letters I'd written her.

Each birthday, Valentine's, Christmas, and anniversary I had either written her a letter or designed a card for her. I dug deeper. These weren't just from after our wedding; I saw the familiar Quantico mailing address—letters from when I was away, back when we were still dating. She had kept them all. Dozens and dozens and dozens of letters and cards.

I felt like a sponge racked for its last drop. I'd thought that I'd given my all for her. Why hadn't it been enough? Would I ever have enough to give to someone?

Looking down at my hand, I stared at my wedding ring. Pulling it from my finger, I turned it, studying the cold reflection of the white gold, two parallel lines etched in the wide band. I looked at it, detached, like a curious observer. My hand felt naked. I wanted to put it back on for the security it had given me, the reassurance it had stood for: that I was loved, that I belonged, that the uncertainty of trying to get to know a stranger no longer applied to me. Yet here I was, back at square one. The thought of finding someone, of starting the process again, turned my stomach. I couldn't imagine loving anyone else. I dropped the ring into the back of a dresser drawer and slammed it shut.

Merry Christmas.

5

NEW YEAR'S

The New Year's Eve party was packed. Hunkered at a circular table in the corner with my friends, I surveyed the crowd. The noise level was approaching unbearable as everyone grew rowdier the closer it got to midnight. I still struggled being around large groups of people, but this was one night for certain I didn't want to be sitting in that empty house alone. In my peripheral line of sight, I noticed two girls across the room looking my way. It wasn't the first time that evening.

I flashed back to a conversation I'd had with my big brother, Abe, a couple months earlier. Even though I had him beat by a couple inches, I still referred to him as big brother, or Father Abraham, depending on the situation. I had left my office to meet him at Moe's. Over burritos, we'd caught up on life, and then he had dived into the deep end.

Rubbing his goatee, he set his cup down. "So how are you doing, Ikes?" Nicknames tended to stick with me.

I never minded when he asked me this question, because I always knew that he actually cared about the answer, no matter how long it took for me to share it. He was one of the strong influences that had helped keep me from going off the rails.

I pulled at my straw. "It's hard, man. You think it's tough staying pure before you get married."

He nodded ruefully.

"Well, try going from being married to single again. It sucks. I mean, really sucks."

"I'm sure."

I leaned back, trying to find the right words. "I mean, I'm still a red-blooded guy with my physical drive intact, but—"

"You're single now."

"Yeah."

Sunlight reflecting off a passing car blinded him for a moment. He rubbed his eyes and paused before continuing. "Are you thinking about another relationship?"

I didn't mean to, but I laughed out loud. A couple ladies in the next booth looked over at me.

"No way. I mean, do I want the physical part of it? Sure, who wouldn't? But as far as the trust goes, forget it. I don't trust anyone anymore. I wouldn't trust a woman as far as I could throw her."

He smiled at my lame attempt at a joke. "That's kind of what I figured, and I just want you to be careful. I'm not preaching at you."

I grinned, "Could've fooled me, youth pastor."

"Touché, but seriously, people look at you—girls look at you. I've seen it. I can't imagine how hard it is; just be careful, bro."

I dropped the humor. Leaning across the table, I let some of the pain slip. "Sometimes I don't care. God says that all things work together for good for those who trust Him. Do you call this 'good?' Because I sure don't. What's the point? I'm alone; no one cares how I respond."

"It may be years before you know why He let this happen. You may never know. As hard as it sounds, you're gonna have to accept that."

He was trying to empathize, I could see it in his eyes, and I appreciated it, but the deadness just seemed too big.

"And there are people watching you. Not the way that I was talking about earlier. I've had people tell me what an encouragement you've been."

I snorted, "Just being brutally honest, but I don't care. God could have used someone else to be their little illustration."

He settled back in his chair rubbing his chin again. "I'm sorry I don't have all the answers, bro. Just know I'm always thinking of you."

———

The raucous music interrupted my memory.

11:57.

I crossed the room to refill my glass. Pausing at the bar, I sensed the figure behind me even before I felt the hand on the small of my back. I tensed. I've never been a really touchy person, and my stint in the Marines seemed to have expanded my need for personal space. My mantra for anyone outside of a personal relationship was "If I can reach you from where I'm standing, you're too close." And at this point, my personal relationship quota stood at a frigid zero.

I turned to find one of the girls who had been watching me earlier practically in my glass.

The crowd began a deafening countdown, "Ten, nine, eight…"

Using the excuse of the noise to lean in further, she asked, "Are you with anyone?"

I leaned back and looked at her. Time slowed. The question slid between my ribs like a knife blade. Didn't she see the emptiness in my eyes? Didn't she realize that there was only one person I wanted to be with? Weren't girls supposed to be the intuitive ones?

I felt sick inside. She was the personification of every other person celebrating this New Year's without a care in the world, grabbing strangers to kiss, singing "Auld Lang Syne," shouting out celebratory wishes. I wanted to carve the smiles off every face, wanted to scream at the world to stop.

She put her hand on my chest and smiled at me. I took a long deliberate sip from my glass and studied her: thin and well-formed, voluminous dark eyes, delicate diamond pendant accentuating the plunging neckline of her green cocktail dress. Close. Too close. Her perfume taking over my senses. It would be so easy just to forget the pain for a few hours.

I looked over her head at the crowd, so carefree, so happy, so empty. Leftover Christmas lights still lined the ceiling, glowing like dizzy fireflies. I wanted to belong, to have someone to go home with, not endure this sucking void that pulled at me. I just wanted to stay a little longer. I felt the warmth of her body against mine.

I knew I'd only drifted for a second, but it felt like hours.

"I have to go."

Elbowing my way through the crowd, I slammed the door open, the little bell jingling angrily. Snow flurries gusted along the sidewalk, chasing hurrying couples intent on finding retreat from the chill. Pulling my jacket open, I leaned against the icy façade of a brick building. Slowly I felt the heat of the party dissipate, and I let my ragged breath grow even in the quiet night air. I had been so close to— What was happening to me?

Half a year, and the pain was still so raw. When was the healing supposed to start? God was a million miles away.

Silence. Nothing but the muted throb of music emanating from various parties along the street. Shadowy figures scurried to cars. Even the moon was absent. I kicked at a rock.

What do you want to hear, child? I never promised that your life would be filled with happiness. Only that I would never leave you. Even when the night is all around you, the blackness so thick you can feel it, the pain so real you can smell it, I will always be at your side. People will fail you, betray you, lie to you, leave you, but I never will. I will be the one constant point in your storm.

Eyes closed, I breathed deeply as my equilibrium began to right itself.

I had to get your attention. You had completely lost sight of Me. No one heals at the same pace. Everyone is different. The path I have chosen for you will be unlike anyone else's. But someday you will look back and accept that what I have allowed was what you needed.

I contemplated that before burrowing my hands into my coat pockets and turning to make my way down the empty street. I felt as if I had stepped into a scene from *The Book of Eli*.[1] Surrounded by darkness, I trudged along, driven by a voice that only I could hear, bearing a burden that was mine alone.

Ahead in the distance, the moon was rising.

6

DEPLOYMENT

I loved Sundays. Standing shoulder to shoulder with friends worshiping, feeding my battered soul. So often my church family gave me the support that I needed to keep me holding on through the seasons of pain.

This week I was excited because I knew that Kate was in town. Brannon had just shipped out on his year-long deployment, and she had come down to visit her family. Leaving the end of the early service at church, I rolled down my windows and enjoyed the brisk spring air as I headed across town to catch her at the end of the late service at our sister campus.

The ending song service was just beginning as I slipped into the back of the dim room. I scanned the backs of heads, looking for the familiar dark blonde hair.

There. She must have gotten in late, because she was standing alone in one of the back rows, eyes shut, hands held out in front of her. I made my way down the side aisle and stepped in beside her.

I gently touched her shoulder. "Emo."

Turning, she looked at me. Surprise, happiness, and pain conflicted in the tears spilling from her hazel eyes as she grabbed me in a hug. I felt the heaving sobs wracking her body, and my heart broke for her. An empty year stretched out before her in which she would never know what might happen to her husband. Anger smoldered inside me at evil men doing evil things that required spouses to suffer while their lovers fought battles on the other side of the world. They didn't deserve this. They were only months into their young marriage, and now they had this battle to face. I hated it. But I knew that in the darkness of their separation, a light of hope still shone. They expected to be reunited. No such light existed for me.

I didn't say anything, just held her until the crying subsided, and suddenly I was standing in my grandma's neighborhood on a warm April night six years earlier. We'd just been notified that our entire unit would be deploying for a year. They had told us, "Go and tell your family and friends. Get ready."

Sunday evenings at church after my drill weekends, Grandma always asked if I heard anything about being deployed. The answer had always been the same, but not this time.

I shook my head slightly. I wanted to tell *her* first.

Grandma understood. I saw the worry, but she would wait.

After supper we went for a walk; her hand felt perfect in mine. She knew that something was wrong. She could read me so well. I broke the news as best I knew how. I hated hurting her, hated it like nothing else. Watching the fear and sadness welling up in those dark-brown eyes, I held her while her mascara stained dark patterns onto my shirt. I couldn't imagine a world without her.

"Promise you'll come back."

I sensed the words more than heard them, muffled into my chest.

Four weeks later, in true Semper Gumby form, we were notified that Marine units from the West Coast were being pulled instead of ours.

"We're not going. Yet."

Since my options were suddenly wide open, I took the opportunity to sign on for a six-month tour in Quantico while she finished school. That separation was difficult for us, but there were still weekends when we could be together and phone calls when we couldn't. I could only imagine the pain of deployment on the other side of the globe, where death was just one mistake away.

Kate had calmed down by the time the last song began. Standing with my arm around her, we sang "It Is Well with My Soul." As we reached the first chorus, I felt her shudder and lean into me.

The final chorus filled the room, and she was no longer the only one crying. I ached for that day when every relationship would be made new, when we would not only be reunited with loved ones but also with Him. Every wrong would be made right, all would be perfect. No more tears, no more loneliness, no more suffering.

Long after the service ended and Kate had taken some time to reconnect with all her friends, I walked her out to her car.

"Thanks for coming and sitting with me."

I grinned. "Friends don't let friends sit alone in church."

She laughed, but the fleeting happiness died quickly. The pain I'd seen so many times in the mirror looked up at me. We stepped aside to let a car past us.

"I know you've got a full schedule with your weekend trip here, but I'm glad I could spend a few minutes with you. I know this year's going to be hard, really hard. Maybe God's allowed my situation to happen so that I'd better understand how to pray for you guys while you're separated."

She was blinking. I knew that it wasn't because of the afternoon sun. She was a strong girl, so much like her sister. The voice that responded was surprisingly small.

"Thanks, Istra. You mean so much to us."

I put my hands on her shoulders and waited for her to look at me. "And I'm promising you that I'm going to write him often."

"That'll mean so much to him. He's really down sometimes. He doesn't want me to know, but I can tell. It's crazy what you find out about yourself, isn't it, when you lose the one person you love more than anything in the world?" She leaned against her car and dropped her head.

Her question hung in the air between us. I didn't know how to answer.

"A year's a long time, but I know you guys. You're both fighters. You're going to be all right."

"I hope so," she whispered.

I gave her one last hug before helping her into her car. Her small convertible slowed at the corner as she stopped to give me one final smile and wave. I waved mechanically, smiling with a warmth I didn't feel, and watched as she rounded the corner and disappeared.

7

SUMMER

One of the things I was painfully reminded of over and over again was the fact that people who knew me often didn't know about the separation. Most of the time I could sense impending awkwardness and drop some hint that would tip them off to what was happening, but other times there was simply no way around it. During those moments I felt like the slightly overweight woman who is asked when her baby is due. There's that deer-in-the-headlights moment when the other person realizes what they've asked as you rack your brain to try to come up with a way to politely put them at ease while at the same time you want to cuss them out.

I was sitting at my desk at the printing company where I now worked, wrapping up my daily reports as the last of my bindery employees headed out. Across the desk beside me, my shipping guy, Heath, was also finishing his paperwork.

When I had started in my position as the bindery manager, a bunch of people had jokingly called Heath and me brothers. I guess we did look similar with our tall, wiry frames and reddish-blonde hair. We had hit it off from day one. I found that I could trust him to handle any job I assigned; his languid style belied the amount of work he could accomplish. Always ready to crack a joke or play a prank, his antics kept the senior management in stitches.

I asked him about some adventure he was planning with his girlfriend. The conversation gradually died off, and I had turned my focus back to my computer screen when his voice broke through my typing.

"Did something happen with you guys?"

"Huh?"

I hadn't really heard him, still focused on keying in the day's numbers.

"I just noticed that you took her picture down. I figured something must have happened."

He had my full attention now. He sat quietly, eyes unfocused, staring through his own screen.

"You never talk about her anymore."

The weight of the day pressed down on my shoulders. I rubbed my neck, trying to relieve the tension.

I looked over at him. "She left me last summer."

He nodded, still silent. I waited.

"My mom left a few years back."

Sadness invaded me. This guy, always so upbeat, bore a pain that he'd never shared with me. The loss of a parent to divorce—my mind teetered on the edge of the rabbit hole, imagining endless questions, pain, and confusion that a young guy would experience. The familiar anger simmered below it all. Didn't people understand how many others got hurt? Didn't they care? How do you abandon your own flesh and blood?

"I'm sorry, man."

He looked up. "It's been a while. My dad and I get

along okay. You just never really see it coming, you know? I remember how you always used to talk about her, had her picture up, then—nothing."

He scanned the dark bindery, letting the silence fill in words that neither one of us felt like saying.

"Do you ever get mad?"

He was still looking off in the middle distance, giving me space, time, letting me off the hook if I wanted.

"Yeah."

I wanted to throw out a glib response like I did with most people. Keep the loss as far away as possible. But I couldn't with him—we'd both been wounded. I owed him honesty.

"I read this quote one time: 'The pain never disappears. It simply explodes less often.'[1] That's what I focus on when I get angry. I can't let myself sit around thinking about it, otherwise it just eats at me. Kinda why I've got to just be going, going, going all the time. The moments when I'm pushing the edge—that's when my mind is engaged in something else. It buries the pain."

"Makes sense."

He pushed back from his desk and slid on his sunglasses, then stopped. He half-started to speak, but I guess he thought better of it.

After a pause, he simply said, "See you tomorrow."

Turning, he made his way out the door into the afternoon sun. I sat watching him go. Finally, I pulled myself back to my monitor. The reports weren't going to run themselves.

As the bindery and shipping manager at the company, I was tasked with keeping the machinery functioning. Any necessary repairs or maintenance issues fell to me to schedule. One of my favorite technicians always loved catching up with me after his visits. Following a two-day work trip, Tommy was packing his tools and preparing to hit the road. Stopping by my desk, he dropped off his paperwork and torpedoed me before I had the chance to react.

"How's that beautiful wife of yours?"

Her picture had been my computer wallpaper, and during one of his first visits, he'd noticed. A big family guy himself, he had immediately wanted to know all about her.

I sensed Heath stiffen at his desk. I took a second, hating to drown the conversation with this guy who was always so kind to me.

"She left. Last year actually."

He took a small step back, a panicked look in his eyes, as he fumbled for a response. I may as well have pulled a pipe wrench from under my desk and smashed him upside the head.

I preempted the response he was struggling to find.

"It's okay, Tommy. Really."

After several such moments like this, I was becoming more adept at restoring balance to conversations.

"It's just... I—I'm really sorry. I didn't know."

I could tell that he wanted to say something, anything. He wanted to know. He wanted to help.

"Seriously. Don't feel bad about it. I appreciate your thoughts."

That wasn't as awkward as the situation I found myself in a few weeks later. I had gotten a new intern in my department and was using him in shipping to lighten Heath's load. He wasn't the strongest worker. At times, I had to go behind him to make sure that stuff got done or that a pallet scheduled for Ohio didn't end up in Illinois. Unfortunately, I was too late on that one.

A driver from the freight company I'd worked at a few years previously pulled in to make a pickup. Seeing me on the dock, he picked his way through the pallets and headed my way.

"Isaiah! I didn't know ya worked up here. All of us drivers miss ya like crazy." He grabbed my hand in a double handshake, his big black ones swallowing mine, pumping up and down, thick Southern accent pouring like molasses. "Dispatch just ain't the same since ya left. Still don't know how ya managed to keep us all goin' all the time."

I smiled, remembering the chaos of the dispatch terminal.

"Great to see you too, Bill. How's your wife? Better, I hope?"

Pushing his sunglasses farther back on his head, he adjusted his headset. "Yeah, she's good. She's doin' real good. Man, it's great to see ya. How 'bout you? Any kids yet?"

Nailed again.

I could pick my way through a booby-trapped forest on night ops, but put a guy in front of me armed with a conversational sledgehammer, and I'm blind as a bat. I should have anticipated a question, any question, at some point. Bill's inquiry shouldn't have been a surprise, but it was.

I was scrambling for what should have been a simple answer when my intern's head popped up from behind a pallet.

"Isaiah doesn't have any kids—he's not even married."

I was calculating just how hard I could throw my clipboard at him when I saw Heath at the edge of the dock. Rolling his eyes, he pantomimed drawing a gun from an invisible holster. Putting it to his head, he pulled the trigger and collapsed out of sight.

Turning back to Bill, I patted him on the shoulder and directed him off the dock toward my desk.

"No kids yet. Someday maybe."

Sensing his confusion, I diverted quickly. "Give me a second while I grab your paperwork."

After Heath finished loading him up, I sent Bill on his way. Standing at the empty bay door, I still felt off balance. Leaning against the dock door, I wearily rubbed my eyes.

Heath pulled up on the forklift and jumped down beside me.

"Real smooth," he muttered under his breath.

"Yeah."

We watched the tail of the trailer disappear around the corner of the building. He pulled the bay door closed before hopping back onto the forklift. He paused beside me.

"You handled that pretty well. For a minute there, I thought you might peg him with your clipboard."

"Just about. Thanks for the diversion."

"That's why you pay me the big bucks."

It was one of those times when we both just had to laugh.

The intern didn't last long.

8

PROTECT

"I love having Isaiah around," my friend said as we waited for the last car to clear the crosswalk. "When he walks, it looks like he's about to attack something."

With the street clear, my group of friends made the turn onto downtown Main Street and headed for a restaurant, where we planned to catch a football game. I pulled my collar up against the chill of an early fall evening and found myself smiling at her comment.

My protective instincts had manifested themselves at a young age. When my two brothers and I were still in elementary school, we had moved into the basement bedroom.

Our basement had two sides: the bedroom side and the unfinished side, which housed the washer, dryer, and utility sink. An open doorway led from the bedroom into the unfinished side, and at night the sounds of the creaking stairs, flexing pipes, and dripping sump pump played havoc with the overactive imaginations of little boys.

As we prepared to set up our beds, my younger brother, Noah, immediately claimed the spot farthest from the open door. Abe, our fearless oldest brother, looked at me and said, "I'm not sleeping by the door." And so my duty as protector began.

Each Saturday, Dad and Mom went out for date night. They generally returned before we went to sleep, but one night when the three of us went to bed, they still hadn't gotten back.

"*Bang! Bang! Bang!*" The crash of noise from the ground-level window wells above our heads jarred us all awake.

I heard Noah first. "What was that!"

"I don't know," whispered Abe. "Isaiah, go see what it is."

Like I said, fearless.

I grabbed a baseball bat and headed for the stairs. Behind me, I heard my brothers following. When I reached the living room, I decided to take a peek out the front window before heading to the door. Abe and Noah appeared from the kitchen armed with assorted butcher knives.

"*Bang! Bang! Bang!*" We all jumped.

Standing between the curtain and the window, I could make out a dark form bent down near the basement window wells. I breathed a sigh of relief. "It's Dad and Mom."

When we finally let them in, we found out that their garage-door opener had died, and somehow they didn't have their house key with them. The only thing Dad could think of was to bang on our window. I'm sure we made a hilarious sight standing there in our pajamas, hair awry, holding our motley assortment of weapons.

I wouldn't say that my time in the Marines heightened my protective instincts but rather gave me more tools to serve those instincts. After we got married and were looking for a studio space for her business in one of the developing areas downtown, I decided it was time for both of us to get our concealed-weapons permits. If I couldn't be there to protect her, I wanted to make sure that she could protect herself. When we had our permits in hand, I had her carry my .40 with her at her studio. The size of the handgun made it too hard for her to conceal, so she wore it openly when her studio was unlocked. It made me smile to walk in and see her working with the pistol on her hip. Eventually, I found a small .380 and switched with her.

When we were out together, I was the one who carried. Because of my slender build, I found that the easiest way for me to conceal my weapon was to wear a belly-band holster that allowed me to carry the pistol in the small of my back. This made for some hilarious moments when someone would give me a hug. Things would normally go something like this: "Are you okay? Are you wearing a back brace?"

"Uh, no, that's my handgun."

It was a great conversation starter.

My in-laws adjusted to my mindset pretty quickly, the only real hiccup coming when they arrived in town to stay with us one weekend. The morning after they arrived, we sat around enjoying a Saturday breakfast, and I asked how they had slept.

"Pretty well," my father-in-law answered, "except that during the night I woke up and had to use the restroom. For some reason I thought that if I got up and walked past your room, you might forget that we were staying here, and you might come out and shoot me, thinking I was someone who'd broken in." He started laughing, "I ended up just peeing out in the backyard. Seemed like a good idea at the time."

Walking down Main Street, my friends and I were nearing the restaurant where we planned to watch the game when I looked in a passing window and did a double take. I felt my blood pounding in my ears. "Hey, you guys, go ahead and get a table. I've got something that I need to take care of."

I waited for them to move off before I backtracked to the window I had just looked through. I couldn't believe it. It was *her.* Her hairstyle was different, but I'd have recognized her anywhere. She was sitting with a guy I'd never seen. As she pushed her hair back behind her ear, I saw that she wasn't wearing a ring. I stood in the shadow of a metal street sign watching. After a couple minutes, I saw him sign the check, give her a kiss on the cheek, and head for the door.

Everything inside me went still, and the surrounding downtown noises faded. I pulled my jacket collar up around my face as he turned out of the restaurant and headed in the opposite direction from where I stood. I checked once more; she was still sitting inside with her back to me.

I caught up to the guy just as we were about to pass a dark alley between two sports bars. He looked to be an inch shorter than I was, but I guessed that he had ten pounds on me. I looked over my shoulder. The closest people were about twenty yards away and deep in conversation.

I dropped a hand on his shoulder. "Hey man, do you have the time?" Before he could answer, I jerked him into the alley and spun him behind a dumpster.

"What the—"

My first punch caught him square in the solar plexus. His breath came out in a chopping huff, and his right arm instinctively shot out at me. I moved with an almost clinical detachment, the result of dozens of hours of hand-to-hand combat drills. I threw a quick forearm block just before grabbing his wrist and pulling it across my body to my opposite shoulder. This off-balanced him while moving me in close to his unprotected flank. I landed two vicious kidney shots, and he dropped to his knees in a spasm of pain. Pivoting on the wet pavement, I brought my knee around and caught him flush behind the ear. He dropped like a wet sandbag, his teeth clicking as he hit the ground face first.

I stood over him, shaking with adrenaline and rage, feeling strangely alive. It had been so easy. The training I'd received all those years ago flooded back as if it had only been last week. I'd spent years wearing my "nice face" in front of my family and friends, all the while knowing the caged animal I held inside. I felt like Jekyll and Hyde, never able to fully explain the things I knew I was capable of. People are inherently curious about what the military trained us to do, but I found that they didn't honestly ever *really* want to know.

Rifling through his jacket, I removed his wallet and phone to make the scene look like a random mugging. I crushed the phone before tossing both it and the wallet into separate dumpsters. I heard a groan as he started to come around. Staring down at him, I wondered who he was. I couldn't blame him, really. I would have pursued her too if I had thought she were single. As that thought went through my mind, the rage came back. I lined up my boot for a kick…

The text alert buzzed in my pocket. "We got a table. Where are you?"

I turned, confused for a moment, as several people pushed past me on the sidewalk. I found myself still at the window, looking in at him and her, both still sitting inside. As they laughed, she turned toward the street, and I saw her face clearly—a face I had never seen before.

It wasn't her.

9

DEATH

The text alert chimed again, breaking through my sleep. Rolling over, I fumbled with my phone and struggled to bring the screen into focus.

3:22.

"Grandma is Home."

Setting the phone down, I stared up through the blackness. Where had the time gone? Memories flooded back, pouring over each other, blurring together. Grandma. A sad smile pulled at my cheeks. She'd been so much more than that to me. Her friendship had become an integral part of my life during my college years. She had hounded my brothers and me incessantly. She had been a matchmaker without rival. She'd had that rare ability to embarrass us to death while innocently acting as if she had no idea what she was doing. But for all her jokes, she never passed up a chance to sit and talk with us. Minutes. Hours. Whatever.

It had never ceased to amaze me how in tune she'd been with what I was going through. You'd think a grandma wouldn't have a clue; but my grandma did. What made her even more impressive was the fact that she'd never had boys of her own. It was almost as if God had known that I'd needed someone with a lifetime's worth of smarts to help me keep my head out of the sand, even though I hadn't always been bright enough to follow her advice. She had been there, ready to listen, in the good times and the bad. God had endowed her with the remarkable gift of being able to bring each situation back into a perspective that included Him. So many times I had lost sight of that.

She had me in absolute fits at times, like the weekend she asked me to come help her paint. I walked in to find her, paintbrush in hand, standing on top of the sink in her bathroom, edging in the border of the ceiling.

"Grandma! What are you doing? Normal grandmas don't do that—they call their grandsons!"

She just laughed at me. "You're only as old as you act."

I treasured that feisty, spontaneous side of her, and it tore me up to see her losing her independence and strength in the battle with cancer. As her strength waned, I noticed that heaven became more and more a topic of our conversations. I knew that she looked forward to reuniting with Grandpa, but it was more than that. She wanted to be with her Savior.

The agonizing battle took its toll on her. There were times when she was overwhelmed by the pain and depression. Sitting in the hospital with her one night, surrounded by beeping monitors and IVs, I did the only thing I knew to do: I held her hand and prayed. The small whimpering body in the bed was nothing like the friend who had laughed and cried with me over the years. I didn't want to lose her, to lose the relationship that meant so much to me. But I wanted her to be free.

As I sat with her, her pastor stopped in to visit. His calm voice always seemed to reflect the truths he loved to teach. Reaching across the bed, he gave me a firm handshake, the flecks of gray at his temples glinting in the cold fluorescent light marking a quiet maturity belied by his young features.

He smiled down at Grandma. "I don't want to keep you long, June, but I wanted to stop in and check on you."

He spent a few minutes in small talk with her before standing to leave. Turning, he asked if he could pray for us. Grandma smiled wanly and nodded.

"Father, there's nothing easy about what's happening here. Both of my dear friends are dealing with their own pain right now. But You told us that the sufferings that we experience now are nothing compared to the glory that You will reveal to us in eternity. Thank You for walking through this journey with each of them."

I heard Grandma's murmured amen from the bed beside me. Behind my eyelids I felt the familiar burn as the knot rose in my throat.

"Make Yourself real to each of them. Be the source of their love and their relief, and be their refuge. Let them turn to You and only You for the rescue that they desire."

Long after he left, I still sat in the dim room. The ragged wheezing from the bed was the only noise accompanying the hum of the hospital machines. Death was no stranger to me. Years earlier I had lost one of my closest friends.

"Stratton."

The envelope whipped through the air, banking at the last moment. Snider, my rack mate, snatched it and passed it across to me.

The smell of Aqua Velva, rubbing alcohol, and shave lotion mixed with the underlying musk of sweat in the squad bay. Evening mail call with our senior drill instructor provided the closest thing to being relaxed that we ever experienced—just so long as we hadn't done anything to particularly aggravate our other DIs while he was absent.

Turning the letter over, I saw that it was from Dad. My brow wrinkled. He hadn't ever sent me two letters in the same week.

"Stratton."

Two more letters arrowed at my head. This time I caught one. My squad leader, Langford, hauled in the other and flipped it my way.

Abe? Mom? What the… ?

Impatiently, I waited for Staff Sergeant Golden to finish his nightly talk before releasing us to our brief evening free time. Plopping down on my footlocker, I ripped open Abe's letter.

"I'm sure by now that you've heard about Justin…"

Everything stopped. A buzzing sound filled my ears. I stopped reading and immediately tore open Mom's letter.

"Dearest Isaiah, if you haven't read your dad's letter yet…"

My fingers were shaking as I picked up the final letter. Opened it. Read it.

"… accident… climbing… Justin… rotten tree… dead…"

The room skewed. Evening sunlight streaming through the windows canted and fractured. We went to sleep early during qual week. Reveille sounded at 0345 to ensure that we were on the rifle range in time to begin firing the moment that the sun broke the horizon.

Dropping my head between my knees, I hugged my legs and rocked back and forth.

My best friend. Dead. He'd died a week ago. He was already in the ground, and I hadn't been there.

I had to pull it together, had to focus. Qual day was tomorrow, and if I screwed up, there was the possibility of being dropped in training, of being sent to another platoon, of graduating late. I had to compartmentalize, to separate from the pain, but I just wanted to scream. How? *How?*

We were better than that. Justin wouldn't have made a mistake. We had done crazy stuff, but we weren't stupid. We had taken our arborist work seriously.

After lights out, I did something I'd never done before: I swung down from my rack, and in the settling darkness of the squad bay, I walked up to the DI's hut. From the corner of my eye, I noticed curious faces following my progress.

Miller, the perpetual platoon screwup, was on fire watch. I glared at him, and he beat a hasty retreat to the far end of the squad bay.

Stopping beside the doorway, I slapped the cinderblock wall three times, the sharp echoes bouncing down the highway. My palm tingled from the impact.

"Sir, good evening, Sir. Recruit Stratton requests permission to speak—"

"What, Stratton?"

Stepping through the door, I struck an awkward position of attention in my PT gear and flip-flops. My senior didn't even look up. His shaved head gleamed in the light from the desk lamp. Gillette could have made a fortune using him on their posters. The cuffed sleeves of his perfectly creased utilities stretched over bulging biceps.

"Sir, this recruit received word that—" I swallowed. Still no acknowledgment. "Sir, this recruit's best friend was killed in an accident."

A pause. Slowly, he looked up, and for a fleeting second I saw emotion in his dark eyes. Earlier in the week, he had given me the news that I'd been selected for the honor of marching as Lead Series Guide at graduation. He knew that I wouldn't jerk his chain.

"Would you like to make a call home?"

I nodded, not trusting my vocal chords.

"Do you have a phone card?"

Another nod.

He pointed to the phone in the corner. I jogged back to my footlocker; fighting my shaking fingers, I finally got the combination right and located the card.

"You okay, Stratton?" Snider whispered from the bottom rack.

I just shook my head and snapped the lock closed.

As I punched in the long string of digits, I glanced at the clock, wondering if they'd be at the house. The connection clicked before the ringing tone that I hadn't heard since the first night on Parris Island echoed through the receiver.

"Hello? This is the Strattons."

My mom's voice sound tinny, far away.

"Mom? It's Str— it's Isaiah."

I hadn't said my own first name in over six weeks. My voice sounded foreign, a half octave lower from the constant strain of shouting at the top of my lungs.

"I just got the letters about Justin."

"Oh, honey! Are you okay? Are you...I—I'm so sorry."

She fumbled into silence.

"Is Dad there?"

She passed the phone to him, and in a few sentences he confirmed what I'd read in the letters. The strange thing was, he'd written his letter days before Mom or Abe, intending for it to reach me first. Somehow all the letters arrived at once.

Justin had been topping a tree, which from all outward signs had appeared completely healthy. When he had cut the top out, the shock of the dropping timber had shattered the base of the tree—it had been completely hollow. It had gone down with Justin in it. When his ground helper had gotten to him, he was already dead, killed on impact.

Friday the thirteenth, 2001.

He was nineteen.

Justin, Stephen, and I had been inseparable, "triplets from different mothers." We had worked landscaping together for several summers and become like peas in a pod. We had known each other as others rarely did, sharing a quiet chemistry people had to experience to understand.

Justin was one of my heroes. I had seen his devotion to Christ; he had been intense about his walk with God, but a person really had to know him to understand the depth of his friendship with his Savior.

Each summer at the anniversary of the accident that took his life, I have made the journey to visit him. Standing on the quiet mountainside surrounded by the hushed nature that he loved, I have asked the same questions: Why did you get taken? Why not me? I looked up to you so much—you had so much to offer in life. Is that why He chose you, because He didn't want to wait for your fellowship with Him to become perfect?

I've stood there and waited, but, just as it was in life, his answer has been silence. I have almost felt him looking at me with his wry smirk, shaking his head. Wondering at my impatient need for answers.

Three of us. The thought never leaves me. If I hadn't been gone that summer, there's a 33 percent chance that I would have been topping that tree. That I would have been the one taking the fall. So many times I've wished that I could have traded places with him.

My visits to his grave always end the same way. I turn and leave, promising to be back the next year. He never responds. He doesn't have to. We understand each other.

A catch in the labored breathing pulled me back. Scooting closer, I asked Grandma if she was okay.

"I can't sleep. Keep thinking about Abe and Liz."

I rested my head on the bed. I was so tired. The fall months had delivered a wicked one-two punch for our family. My brother Abe and his wife Liz had been praying for a little girl and were ecstatic when they had found out they were pregnant. The excitement only intensified when they'd found out they were having a girl. But some abnormal test results had caused concern, and the doctor had recommended them to a specialist. More tests had followed, and the news had come back: There was a problem with the baby. She most likely wouldn't make it, and if she did, there would be serious physical problems.

I had watched with a broken heart while my brother and sister-in-law rode an emotional roller coaster. Their little girl was a fighter. At each checkup, the doctors would gently caution that she probably wouldn't last much longer, but Shiloh kept fighting. Abe and Liz both soldiered on, but I knew that when they were alone, away from everyone else, the real pain hit. Parents shouldn't have to plan for their child's funeral. I found myself getting bitter for them.

Standing with my family at my brother's church, we sang one of my favorite songs, "In Christ Alone." Looking down at the lyrics, the weight of what we were singing almost choked me. All I could think of was the ending of two lives: one barely started, the other full and long, but both so beautiful.

My aunt, who had watched her mom fight the battle with cancer, stood by my sister-in-law, tears rolling down both of their faces as they claimed the promise of the rescue that would come someday.

Grandma's funeral service was beautiful. The outpouring of love and the testimonies of her life spoke volumes about the woman who had impacted so many lives.

But undercutting the whole service was my own throbbing wound. I had thought it was hell going to weddings as a separated person.

I was wrong.

Funerals are worse. Exponentially worse.

I looked from side to side. My brothers with their wives, my parents, my uncles and aunts, and then me. I wanted *her* with me. I hated standing there alone, no one to hold against me, no one to share the pain with. My partner. My lover.

But something else was different on this occasion as well: this time there was no raging grief, there were no tears, only a dull emptiness in me. No emotion while the eulogies were read, the memories recounted. What was wrong with me? I should have been crying. I had lost one of my dearest friends. Where were the tears?

None came.

After a short graveside service, my family huddled up, giving Abe and Liz time to visit Shiloh's grave, which was nestled a couple hundred yards from Grandma's resting spot. Shiloh had passed a little over two weeks earlier. I watched them. This strong, athletic, young couple now looking so broken, shattered by what they'd experienced. My parents, younger brother and his wife, little sister, and I gathered around them. Wrapping my arm around my big brother's shoulders, I watched him cry as I'd never seen him cry before.

The tiny gravestone looked almost fake to me, overturned dirt still crumbling near my shoes. This didn't make sense. I looked up to him, respected him, loved him. They'd done nothing to deserve this. The unfairness of it all ate at me.

"All things work together for good for those who love God."

Really?

10

DIVORCE

Worst day of my life.

Standing at my closet, I felt lost. What do you wear to get divorced? Something serious, I guess. I wanted someone to tell me, to make the decision for me. I settled on a dark shirt, jeans, and a blazer. Looking in the mirror, I tried to figure out what was going on in the pit of my stomach.

Nerves? Really? In college I had acted in theatre productions in front of thousands of people, and I was getting nervous over this?

Part of my heart was dying today. I would cut myself some slack.

Walking into the family court waiting room, I felt as if I'd stepped onto another planet. Tired moms held wailing kids. In the corner a guy in a wifebeater picked up a little boy. Pulling him onto his lap, he rested his chin on the child's buzzed head, the tattoos on his heavily muscled arms incongruously belying his tenderness.

Kids.

We'd talked about them. Wanting to wait a few more years, but knowing they'd come eventually. Always joking about what beautiful babies we'd make. How they'd play sports, grow up, get in trouble, drive us crazy.

But they'd be ours.

Our kids.

Several weeks earlier, I'd stopped at a restaurant just so I could be around people. Sitting at my table waiting on my drink, I had looked around the room. A family walking in the door had caught my eye: a middle-aged couple with two girls wearing cross-country uniforms, both probably less than fifteen years old, one brunette, one dark blonde. The easy familiarity between the dad and mom born of years of loving companionship had reflected in the confidence and exuberance of the girls. Athletic yet lanky, they were still growing into the tall bodies they'd been blessed with. For a moment, I felt as if I'd seen the ghost of the children we should have had. All the physical characteristics were there, right down to the long necks and high cheekbones.

In my distraction, I hadn't even realized that I was still looking at them, when the brunette glanced across the restaurant and caught my gaze. Brilliant blue eyes glowing under dark bangs had exuded a quiet seriousness. She blinked a shy smile before turning back to her sister.

Forcing my blurred vision back to my menu, I fought the images.

We should have shared that.

Now they would never exist.

Stepping around the corner, I saw her. For a second, I couldn't believe it. My mind floated out into a disembodied observation mode: I watched as two young adults, looking as if they could have just stepped off a high-fashion photo shoot, stood lost in the unfamiliar chaos. But nothing shook the finality of what the presence of these two people here represented.

I couldn't take my eyes off her. More beautiful than the first day I had seen her all those years ago. My attention had been seized by the stunning brunette freshman standing across the large campus dining room. She had been with someone else then. Now she was alone, and I still couldn't have her. My feet mechanically carried me toward her.

Why did I still love her? Why did I still want her? After all the pain? Was I some kind of idiot to still want this woman who had walked out on me and ripped a gaping hole in my heart? This woman whom I just wanted to grab and hold until I could let her know that everything was going to be okay—that I was here now. That I was here as I had never been before. Didn't she understand that she'd put the color in my world? I'd been lost in the dark since she left. I just wanted her to look at me one more time the way she used to right before she would lean in and lay her head on my chest, knowing that I was going to take care of everything for her. The feel of her body against me. So right. We were perfect.

She stood in front of me.

"Hey."

Sitting in the courtroom, I looked around. There wasn't much to see. The stenographer, bailiff, and us. Sitting on separate sides of the aisle like enemies. Heavy wooden furniture and dark paneling encircled the room. Even the table in front of me carried a depressing weight of finality. A pitcher of water and a glass rested beside the microphone. I wondered how long they had sat there untouched.

The judge entered and took his seat. The motion seemed so natural. Years of repetition. It all felt cheap, casual. Our two lives were ending, and we were just another number on the docket. I wanted to scream, to pick up a heavy wooden chair and throw it, to do something, anything, to make this different. I didn't want to be another faceless statistic.

What gave him the right to tell us that this was over? Who had died and made him God? How could a couple pieces of paper say something that my heart refused to accept? We had dreams. We had plans. I wanted to grow old with her, to make a lifetime of memories together. Didn't he understand that he couldn't do this?

He looked down at us with a quiet firmness in his eyes.

"Is there anything that can be done to save this marriage?"

From across the aisle, I dimly registered her negative response.

You hear about time slowing down, about people's lives flashing before their eyes. I didn't see my life blaze by, but I'm pretty sure time completely stopped at that moment. I wasn't perfect, but who was? I'd never done divorce before. I hadn't known exactly what to do through the journey, but I had fought the only way I'd known how, and nothing had worked. It felt as if I had made even more of a mess with my efforts. I had woken up, but it had been too late.

In a small courtroom a thousand miles below me, a lost guy was looking up at a family court judge, swallowing, trying to get the word out. The one word he would've died not to say.

"No."

Something was terribly wrong. The room tilted, a buzzing static built in my ears. I shook my head.

"...and so I declare..."

I pinched my thigh. Maybe it was a dream, maybe this really wasn't happening, maybe the last year had all been a sick joke and the walls were about to part and show the audience watching this scripted tragedy.

"...motion of divorce has been granted."

The walls didn't move. There was no audience, no joke, nothing. The judge was turning, leaving, disappearing through the side door. This was happening. I looked over, but she was already halfway to the back door, head turned away, and for a second I couldn't picture her face. I couldn't see the high cheekbones, the dark eyes; it was all blank.

I leaned against the table, sensing the bailiff behind me, and then the walls did move. Everything was closing in, suffocating me.

I bolted for the door. Shoving past the people at the front entrance, I rushed out into the sunlight and sprinted across the parking lot after her. Grabbing her shoulder, I whipped her around.

"You should have given me one chance—that's all I asked for, one freakin' chance!"

Her brown eyes widened with shock. She tried to step back, but I had her by both shoulders, my face inches from hers.

"I can still read the pain in your eyes. I've tried to hide mine, but I can't. I want to know that you are aware that you're making the worst mistake of your life right now." My voice and body shook from the adrenaline release of finally speaking my mind. People passed by in the parking lot, not giving us a second glance.

"I don't even know if God cares anymore. I can't even imagine another relationship. All I can think about is the possibility that another person would end up leaving me too. Who the hell can I trust after this?"

My hands dropped from her shoulders. She didn't move, didn't respond. I had never spoken to her like this. I took a half step back before turning one final time.

"You left me, and now I'm leaving you. Not by choice, but because you gave me no option, and now I've got to leave and see if I can go find a place where I can heal."

I noticed her lawyer standing nearby, staring.

"Don't you have someone else's life to go ruin?" I snarled.

The bailiff's hand on my shoulder made me jump. From my seat in the courtroom, I turned and looked back again. She was gone. The bailiff and I were alone except for the haggard man looking back at me through the window.

It took me a second to recognize my own reflection.

11

DOWN

Behind
Bridges smolder
Ignited by
Another.
Restless soul
Lean a shoulder
Into tomorrow.

Standing at the door, I looked back through the empty house. It was so quiet. I turned the lock, stepped outside, and pulled the door shut behind me. In the driveway my truck sat waiting, already packed with everything I'd be taking with me. I'd stripped my life down to the bare essentials, selling off everything that I'd been able to. Selling the house had been a pain with the depressed market, but I was willing to take the financial hit to get the mortgage off my back. To be able to leave. To move. To grieve somewhere else.

I'd found a roommate in Nashville almost immediately after the divorce and made plans to move as quickly as I could. The memories of the past ten years in Greenville were too much. I was uprooting and moving to a place where I knew practically no one: the agent I had worked with a couple years earlier, one family from my church who had relocated there for work, a buddy from the Marines, and oh yeah, a roommate I'd only met once. I was flying blind.

Closing my truck's door, I turned the key in the ignition. Behind me, the empty house looked sad. Blank windows regarded me with reproachful disdain, not believing that this was how the beautiful dream of "our first house" was ending: the tree we had planted; the shed we had built that had blown over in a crazy storm only a week after we'd put it up, still dented with the one door that wouldn't close quite right; the new front porch—all of it felt like a sad joke with no punch line.

Reaching up, I adjusted the rearview mirror. The face of a stranger flashed back at me, and, for a second, two dull eyes locked with mine. Foreign, hollow, lifeless. A flash of forgotten happiness, mixed with heartbreak and infinite bitterness.

I dropped the gear shift into drive and pulled away for the last time.

■―――■

Walking around the grocery store, I realized that I knew no one. Absolutely no one. Any time in past years in Greenville, I'd have run into someone I knew by now, but not here.

I embraced the anonymity, the freedom from questions and from those horrible sad looks from people who had no idea what to say. I didn't care; the numbness had overtaken me. A disdainful recklessness seeped into me. What was happening? There was a time when I would have tried to figure it out, but now all I wanted was to forget.

Sitting in the dark parking lot, I pulled out my phone and absentmindedly played with it while my thoughts wandered. No one knew me. I typed in a search for a club. I was going to find a distraction, and I didn't care what it was.

I could feel the pulsing music in my chest before I even got to the thick double doors. A bouncer stepped forward, and I offered my ID. Scanning it, he motioned me past. I couldn't shake the irony. I'd been to clubs several times in the Marines, but always to pick up a buddy, never to go in—and now here I was. I stopped for a moment inside the doorway to get my bearings as my eyes adjusted to the darkness interspersed with lancing lights. A stage dominated the far side of the club. The place was huge. Working my way across the room, I found an empty chair. A girl approached and took a seat on my knee.

"What can I get for you?"

"Just a drink."

She returned a few minutes later, setting the glass on the table beside me.

"Anything else?"

"I'm good."

"You sure? Looking for any particular type?"

"Just give me a few minutes."

"Okay, I'll be around."

Sipping on my drink, I looked around the room, wondering why the others were there. I asked the same question of myself, and in that moment I struggled to answer. I wanted attention—someone to tell me I was desirable and that there wasn't anything wrong with me, someone who wouldn't reject me—even if I had to pay for the attention. I didn't realize that I'd finished my first drink, when a second materialized beside me. A couple girls passed by and gave me questioning glances. I waved them off. The hand on my shoulder let me know that my personal server had returned.

"Listen, I've got a girl for you. Gia just got here, and I'm going to send her over. If you don't like her, no worries, but I'm pretty sure you will." With a wink, she vanished again.

Gia? Where did they come up with the names? I was half expecting her to say "Diamond" or "Angel." I upended my glass. Across the room I could make out a girl winding her way between the tables toward me. Heads turned, following her progress. The initial impression she gave me was of a runway model who had spent the past several years perfecting the art of yoga.

Sliding onto my lap, she draped an arm around my shoulders and murmured in my ear, "Hillary said you needed some company." She smelled as good as she looked.

"I guess you could say that."

Suddenly all that time I had spent wondering why guys went to clubs and spent so much money made sense to me. I knew that it was a show, that it wasn't real, but I didn't care. The attention felt good. I pulled out my wallet.

The weeks coalesced into a blur as I did whatever it took to numb the gnawing pain, to forget the loneliness. Following an evening networking event, I found myself in the lobby bar of one of the downtown hotels. I sat alone, fighting the numbness again. Two seats down the bar, a woman finished a phone call—some work-related affair from what I could gather. I looked back up at the sports news playing on the corner TV.

"Are you from around here?"

I turned. Sliding her phone into her bag, she was looking my way.

"Actually just moved here a couple months ago. You?"

"No. Just flew in for a business seminar. So lame. Thought I was going to fall asleep halfway through today."

"I know the feeling," I laughed. "I've been through some of those. Coffee is a lifesaver."

It was her turn to smile, revealing a sparkling line of perfect teeth. She slid over into the seat next to me, her shoulder pressing against mine.

"So what do you do now?"

"Actor."

"In Nashville? Why aren't you in Los Angeles?"

"You have no idea how often people say that. You'd be surprised how much stuff is filmed around here. Plus, the field isn't saturated. Want to guess how many actors are looking for work in L.A.?"

"Makes sense."

Turning to the bartender, she ordered a drink before hesitatingly asking me, "Are you getting something else?"

"Well, it'd be a bit rude to run off right after we started talking. So that'll be a yes."

The drinks came back, and before I knew it, an hour had passed.

"So I'm staying here, and my flight doesn't leave till early tomorrow afternoon." She pushed a strand of hair behind her ear before resting her hand on my arm. "You want to come up?"

The complete casualness of it jarred me. The unstated declaration that this was what people did. No strings, no relationship, just the here and now. Everything inside me rebelled for an instant, completely refusing to believe that I was contemplating the question. I took a cold look at my past and realized that I didn't care.

I threw a tip on the bar and stood. Tonight I wasn't saying no.

It wouldn't be the last time.

Sunlight glared through the shades as I lay staring at the ceiling of another foreign room. I rubbed my aching eyes.

I had become one of those guys I had always hated, the ones who objectified women. When had I started believing that this would make me feel any better? All I had done was hurt myself and others, but I had been too stupid to see it.

Looking over at the sleeping woman beside me, I felt the self-loathing rising in my throat like bile. Quietly easing out of bed, I pulled on my clothes and slipped out of the room. Walking out of the building, I shivered in the brisk spring morning, then paused, trying to remember where I had left my truck. I knew that something had to change—I couldn't keep going like this. I had finally hit bottom, and it was horrible.

12

TURN

To say that the Gaylord Hotel is gigantic would be a fundamental understatement. It sprawls across acres of land, commanding attention. I'd driven around it a few times before grumpily realizing that there was no way I was going to pay twenty dollars to park. I could walk. Driving back down the long entryway, I finally spied some restaurant parking lots adjacent to the main intersection outside the hotel.

A talented young filmmaker friend of mine was in town for a film festival and competition, and he had invited me to help out with the film project he was shooting. I had met Justin years before in downtown Greenville, South Carolina. He had just crawled out of the Reedy River, soaking wet, followed by his brother, Jordan, who was trailing him with a video camera. The sight was so out of the normal, I couldn't help laughing and had stopped the two of them to find out what they were up to. Turns out that they had been shooting a Bear Grylls spoof. With my passion for acting, we had hit it off right away and stayed in touch over the years.

Justin's talent as a filmmaker was matched by an incredible heart. When his brother Jordan had passed away following a battle with cancer, Justin had become even more passionate about telling truth through film. He had the vision to shoot nuanced performances to tell stories that people would ponder rather than stories that would beat people over the head. I'd had the opportunity to act in a few of his short films, and he and I stayed in touch even after I moved.

I looked up at the hotel again and breathed a prayer of thanks for cell phones. Finding Justin would have been nearly impossible otherwise.

"What's up, man?"

"Hey. I just parked, and I'm walking up to the hotel's entrance, no clue which one. Where are you guys?"

After receiving some sketchy instructions, getting lost in an indoor jungle that rivaled the Amazon rain forest, and making several wrong turns, I finally joined up with the group. I grinned when I walked into the room. There was no question that there were five guys crashing there—five filmmakers, that is. Widescreen monitors, laptops, hard drives, light rigs, pizza boxes, and energy drinks littered the room. A raucous cheer greeted my entrance. I laughed and made the rounds, greeting the team, exchanging bear hugs with friends.

"So when do we start shooting?"

Justin turned from his laptop where he'd been typing. "About an hour. I've got an actor coming into town to help with the shoot, and I want to introduce you to him."

I hadn't realized how much I missed having friends after having spent months by myself in a new city. I relished the energy that came with being on the set of even a short film shoot, and the prospect of connecting with other local actors made it that much better.

After wrapping some establishing shots in one of the lobbies, Justin's phone rang. He answered and gave some directions again. I hoped that his actor friend would have better directional sense in this building than I had.

"That was Torry. Dude, you're going to love him."

We made our way to the site for the next shot, and that's when Torry found us. The initial impression I got was hair. Red hair. Lots of red hair. A big bear of a man with fiery hair matched by a beard of the same color. I was expecting a big booming voice as I shook his hand but was surprised by friendly, intense words that struggled to harness boundless energy. I could tell that this was a guy I'd enjoy being around.

For the next few hours, Torry had us in stitches. His witty comebacks were unbelievable. Everything would be set for a take, and he'd drop a quiet one-liner that had Justin yelling "Cut!" while the rest of us doubled over in laughter.

Before I left I exchanged numbers with Torry, and we made plans to meet up. Grabbing Justin in a hug, I wished him good luck.

"Hurry up and graduate already so we can start making films together."

He rolled his eyes. "I hate school."

"Be cool. Stay in school."

"Shut up!"

I've always loved driving. Something about the freedom of movement, seeing new places, soaking in new experiences. The drive to Sparta, Tennessee, was perfect—clear spring skies overhead contrasted with the crisp green of the mountain pines. Torry had invited me to come out to spend a few days at his place in the mountains. He and I had hit it off after our initial meeting, and our shared passion for film led into hours of interesting discussions. I came to realize that not only was he one of the funniest people I'd ever met, but he was an incredible writer, storyteller, networking genius, and, as I was soon to find, a culinary artist.

He had spent several years in Alaska, penned books, appeared in several films, won multiple writing awards, and even written for *Adventures in Odyssey*. Because he traveled so much, I jumped at the chance to spend a few days with him when his schedule opened up.

Walking into his house, I felt as if I'd stepped into an Alaskan cabin. Rustic decor and a sense of warmth pervaded the atmosphere. Countless moose and bear figurines dotted the walls and shelves. The downstairs was set up to house the numerous guests that passed through, complete with a writing/meeting room. I felt as if I was at home away from home.

Our discussion ranged from film projects to acting gigs before we turned to our shared passion of writing.

"Writing seems more like a release for me, a way to digest pain and hurt, but I feel that I need to do more with it," I told him.

Torry laughed. "No joke. I read some of your short stories. You seriously need to watch some Disney movies or something. Way too much death and pain!"

"It's what I know. It's what I have to say. I can't help it that after what I went through I don't have a notebook full of fluffy fairytales to write. I know that my stuff's dark, but I want people to know that you don't just move on from what I've been through. You're never the same.

"It's like…" An illustration I'd never voiced began to pour out. "It's like identical twins, right? They are born together, they grow together, go to school together, study together. They're identical in every way—physically, mentally, socially. One day, on the way back from a game, they get in a car wreck, a horrible wreck. One brother is ejected, and his arm gets mangled so badly that they have to amputate it."

The words were tumbling over each other; I had to force myself to breathe.

"Years down the road, what's different? They're still brothers, right? Still same brains, same personalities, right? But what's the difference? One of them is missing his freakin' arm! He'll *never* be the same!"

I forced myself back into my chair, trying to calm my breathing. Torry let out a low whistle.

"Sounds like someone's touched that nerve before."

"Yeah, a few times. People just think you're going to move past it, get over it, like a death. But it's different—it's *so* different. Death is a severing that you can't argue with. Divorce is a tearing apart with questions that will never be answered. A friend recently told me that he thought I had moved on, that I was doing better. He didn't realize that I still have a lot of really bad days. I guess I've gotten good at hiding what I'm feeling."

He took a moment to digest that before looking up, and a quiet seriousness shifted his voice. "I get the feeling that you've been through a lot since the divorce. I know that you want to share hope, but you can't guide others to it if you're not on the path yourself."

I studied my coffee, listening to the solid tick of the grandfather clock in the corner.

"Sometimes I wonder what the point is. Does it even matter?"

His eyes were sad, and he hesitated before responding. "God gave you a gift, and He wants you to use it, but you're never going to experience any blessing on your acting or writing as long as you're…" he paused, presumably searching for a delicate way to say the next phrase, "doing things for satisfaction outside of Him."

A warmth flushed my cheeks. We had only been friends for a few weeks, yet Torry had nailed me between the eyes. I hadn't discussed with him any of my recent activities, yet somehow he had picked up on it. So much for my solitary existence. But the words held truth that my heart had already been screaming at me. I had just needed to hear it from someone else.

"There are people out there who need to hear your story, who need to know that they're not alone, that someone else understands what it's like to lose a relationship. But you have to pull your life back on track."

Setting his cup down, he leaned forward in his chair. The sadness was back. "You've been hurt in a way that I don't understand, but I do know that if you look for relief anywhere but in Him, it'll never work."

My hands tightened around my mug, knuckles turning white, tendons tensing in my forearms. The raw hole was opening up all over again.

Child, I designed that hole so that you'd never be able to fill it. You can pour all the distractions the world has to offer into that hole, and it'll still be just as empty as when you started.

I looked up at Torry, sipping his coffee, sitting patiently.

"I've known what you're telling me for a long time. I knew that the stuff I was doing wouldn't really help. I guess I just didn't care."

He waited silently.

"I think…" Shock washed through me as the realization of my true motivation crystallized. "I think I was actually trying to get back at God for what He allowed to happen."

I was stunned. I'd never voiced that. It just broke free; a fragment I'd buried so deeply that I hadn't even realized it existed. I tensed, half-expecting a lightning bolt to crash through the roof, but as the moments slipped by, a feeling of relief flooded through me. The realization of what I'd done, what I'd become, still screamed at me, but now I understood. Every time I'd tried to hurt Him, He'd still loved me. He hadn't gone anywhere. It was I who had left.

The candles on the coffee table sputtered as we both sat digesting the weight of my revelation.

"Talk to Him. People are always going to misunderstand you, but He never will." Torry's words reached out to me.

"I need a few minutes. Think I'll take a drive."

Crossing the room, he gently squeezed my shoulder. "Take all the time you need."

In the evening dusk, I drove in no particular direction. Thoughts jumbled through my brain, fighting for attention. The noise was almost more than I could stand.

He had promised that His Spirit would intercede for me in ways that couldn't be spoken. I wanted that finally. I was ready for Him to take all the things that I was yearning to say. My heart cracked open.

His answer, like so often before, came through the words of the song playing quietly on my stereo. The simple tune of JJ Heller's "Your Hands" enveloped me. I found myself pulling into a deserted grocery-store parking lot, lights just beginning to flicker in the deepening gloom. I slid the control into park and stared down at my trembling hands. Hugging my arms against myself, I leaned back and shook, the emotional jam breaking free in my soul. I surrendered to the pent-up tears from months of buried pain. I cried for myself, for her, for my family, for the ones I had hurt and the ones who had hurt me, for the life that I would never live, but most of all for the One who had always been there, taking every hurt alongside me, reaching wounded hands to catch my battered soul, never giving up, always calling, ready to welcome me back, to welcome me home.

Sobbing, I dropped my head. "It's been such a long time—and I've got a lot to say."

Listen
For it is in those moments
Of deepest silence
I often scream
Loudest.

13

LIVE

The text beeped through on my phone.

12:15 a.m.

Torry. No wonder, that's when the night owl did his best work.

"Check your e-mail."

"What's up?"

"Sending over info on a film you need to audition for. A friend of mine is directing it, and I'll be in it as well. Drama, action, right up your alley. It'd be great to work together."

Seconds later my phone's e-mail notification went off. Thumbing down through the attachment, I had to agree—this did look intriguing. A post-apocalyptic film. I had a few days to submit my video audition. I'd call my agent in the morning to set up a time to film.

The past few months had been a whirl of different auditions—trying out for everything from psychopathic, homicidal rednecks to Elvis impersonators, with a boatload of music videos in between (hello, this is Nashville). Bookings, on the other hand, hadn't been so busy. I was excited to have something in which I would actually have a connection with the minds behind the camera, no matter how small that connection might be.

I spent the next several days preparing for the two roles for which I'd be auditioning. After taping I felt physically exhausted. Nothing to do but wait and see if I heard back.

I loved the feeling of blowing all my energy, throwing it into a character, making him live, breathe, be. Each one had a different story, and though some were easier than others to relate to, each one held some appeal for me.

The e-mail reply finally came. The director and his casting crew had received an overwhelming response to the casting post, and it was going to take longer than anticipated for them to respond with a decision. I felt the old doubt sinking in.

"God, please, will you give me favor on this one? Just one yes. Just a sign that I'm in the right place, that I'm doing the right thing here."

I went back and forth, praying, trying to give it to God and let it go, but in the back of my mind, the thought kept running that it was going to be just another swing and a miss.

Finally, the e-mail:

"We would like for you to come to callbacks in Charlotte. If you can come in person, that would be the best, but if travel is not an option, we can set up a Skype session."

I threw a fist pump.

Skype? Yeah, right. I made plans for the trip. I was going to blow them away.

While I waited to hear back, Torry put me in touch with a producer friend of his. His network connections never ceased to amaze me. When I realized that the producer was in Charlotte, I contacted him about meeting for coffee while I was in town for auditions.

A few days later, he responded, "Sounds great. I'm friends with the director of the film you're auditioning for, and he's having me sit in and help with the casting process. We can grab lunch after your audition."

Double fist pump.

In addition to the characters I had already submitted, they asked me to audition for another character as well. I was thrilled at the extra opportunity.

Walking into the holding room, I took in the other actors. A gray-haired man and a big black guy who easily could have passed as a bouncer. The callbacks were supposed to run all day, and the crew had a bunch of roles to see. I found a corner where I could drop my stuff and began running my lines. Before long that moment that every actor loves and dreads came as the door pushed open and a man with his nose buried in a notebook stuck his head in.

"Isaiah Stratton?"

The nervous adrenaline began pumping in earnest.

I followed him into the audition room and was greeted by a group of people: director, camera man, casting staff—and Cecil, the producer friend of Torry's. They took turns shooting off some questions about my resume.

"You were Bradley Cooper's shoot double?"

"How many years were you in the Marines? Tell us about your weapons training."

"How was it working with George Clooney and John Krasinski?"

After running my first scene, they gave me new direction and had me run it again. Next they gave me a minute to settle into my second character before repeating the process. After wrapping I thanked them all and headed out. Cecil caught up with me in the hall, and we set off to find a place to eat.

Over tacos he gave me feedback from the audition. "They liked you. Especially what you did with the character after they gave you another direction to take things. They believed you."

I was ecstatic. "I know that you know how rare it is to actually hear feedback from what happens in the casting room after we actors walk out. We're always thinking *Did I blow it?* or *I could've done that so much better!*"

He laughed. "I know."

"I'd really love to get a part in this film, not just because it's a job but because of what they're doing with the story—taking a biblical story and putting it in modern, well, post-apocalyptic times. Pretty interesting."

"Yeah, they're going to do it right—the finished project should look great."

"This is exactly why I left a good job to chase a dream that's, more often than not, full of uncertainty. There are stories that need to be told—" I hesitated.

He nodded. "I'm sensing a 'but.'"

"But there are so many people who don't understand this acting life or who throw up walls when they hear what I'm doing. I mean, I was raised to perform. My brothers and I were reciting *The Declaration of Independence* for our relatives at Christmas when we were barely out of kindergarten."

Cecil almost choked on a mouthful of chips and salsa. "Say what?"

"Yeah, my brothers and me, we were pushed, pushed, pushed. Perform, perform, perform. Write, act, sing, be in front of people. And that's what I'm doing, right? It's just that

I'm doing it on film instead of on a stage. I just want to be a light. It's so hard to explain to people who aren't familiar with the industry."

He got the coughing under control. "Sorry, I just had this hilarious mental picture of three tiny boys standing at attention spouting off *The Declaration of Independence*. Did you even understand what you were saying?"

"C'mon, man, I was six. What do you think? Anyway, all I'm trying to say is, I've been doing this all my life. I never felt completely at home in any of my 'normal' jobs, but when I'm on set in front of a camera, I just come alive."

He nodded, "I understand you. From what you've told me of your past, it sounds as if God's put you through the ringer for a reason. You do have a story to tell, and you'll be able to relate to characters in a way that many actors never will."

Folding his napkin, he pushed back his plate and paused for a second. "Embrace the pain, the loss, and the forgiveness; embrace it all. Accept that God has allowed you to walk where you've walked so that someday you'll look back and take that road map and guide others. You will be a light."

"Isaiah!"

I spun around, already extending my arms for the incoming hug, nearly knocking over a brochure stand in the post-church rush. I had decided to swing through South Carolina before heading back to Nashville, and the timing had worked out perfectly for me to spend a Sunday morning at my old church.

"Patti Jo!"

Closer to my parents' age than mine, Patti Jo and her husband had been a perpetual source of encouragement to me during my divorce. They loved pouring into my life.

Releasing me, she stepped back and gave me the up-and-down. "You look great."

"Thanks, I try."

Laughing, she shot back, "No, no, I mean you always do. What I meant was, you look—*happy*. I don't know, something's just different."

I stepped closer to her to avoid a pack of high schoolers that was pouring out the doorway.

"I'm not really sure what to say. I don't feel happier. If you're seeing something different, it's not coming from me." A beautiful smile radiated across her face. She grabbed my arm with her personal-trainer grip and squeezed.

"I know! And that's why it excites me. You're a completely different person from the guy I knew last year or the year before. He's showing through you."

It still didn't make sense to me how I somehow appeared happier when I still felt so beat up on the inside. A confused "thanks" was all I could come up with as she pulled me to the corner of the foyer away from the exiting masses.

"There's something I want to tell you. One of our last conversations has stuck in my head, and I recently heard something that I want to share with you."

I crossed my arms and made a show of bracing myself. "Well, this sounds ominous."

"Stop it," she laughed. "I want to encourage you. Remember when you talked about knowing when you'd be ready to move on? When the void she left would fade?"

"Sure," I shot back, a little more tersely than I wanted to.

She brushed the response aside without hesitating. "Listen to me. That void—it's never going to fade."

"Wow, well, thanks for that." The terseness ratcheted up a notch.

"Isaiah, He allowed her in your life, and you loved her. You loved her so much that you asked her to marry you, to share her life with you. That scar, that void, defines you now, and you have to stop falling into it. What matters now is what you do with the loss. What will you look to?"

I'd never heard the concept framed that way. The dots began to connect. A beautiful picture from my years of tree work filled my mind. I had been preparing to fell a tree one day when I'd noticed a scar running from the ground all the way up the trunk. The tree had suffered a lightning strike years earlier and had survived. The gash had been noticeable before I'd started the job, but it wasn't until after dropping the tree that I'd been able to see the extent of the damage: a dark, knotted pattern in the stump revealed the devastating injury, but years of growth had wrapped around the scar, allowing the tree to grow and thrive.

I shook my head. "But I promised her, I promised God, and I promised myself that I'd love her until death. How do I break that promise?"

She raised her hand to stop me. "You aren't breaking your promise. That promise is a statement of your love. In a way, you will always love her, even through the pain that the memories bring. Just like your brother and sister-in-law will always love their baby, just like your mom and aunts will always love your grandma." The intensity in her eyes was physical. "She will always be part of your story. Accept that. And someday you may meet someone else," her voice grew tender, "or you may not. But if you do, that woman will accept that scar in your life as a sign of just how deeply you loved and are capable of loving." She paused. "And she will embrace you for it."

I didn't need words. I just hugged her, and in that moment a clarity and a stillness that I had yearned for overwhelmed me.

Colors cascaded across the horizon as I chased the setting sun through the Tennessee mountains. There was still so much uncertainty ahead, but the ground beneath me felt solid again. I hooked my anchor into the Rock that had promised always to be there for me, even at my loneliest moments; even in those times, I would still be loved. I could almost feel the physical pressure of a door closing behind me, guiding me into my new journey. That quiet voice that I'd come to cherish promising purpose.

I reached into my glove compartment for my charger. Shuffling beneath the paperwork inside, I felt a small stone. Pulling it out, I recognized the familiar gray rock. I flipped it over.

Hope.

I turned it in my hand, feeling the smooth, worn contours. I smiled.

The wind whistled through my open windows as I drove into the night.

I had stories to tell.

Embrace your scars
Never-dying reminders
That define you
Make you
Beautiful.

AFTERWORD

When I sat down to write this book, I was scared, intimidated. I'm an actor, not some published writer. But through my journey of divorce, I realized how much writing helped me to deal with what I was facing.

I realize that what I've written is only a chapter of my life. I've been asked by some of my early readers for relationship advice, about what I've learned and how I've changed, but that wasn't the goal of this book. Maybe somewhere down the road, I'll write another book.

For now I've embraced this new path that I'm on. I've settled into my new life in Nashville. I've found a wonderful church home and some of the best Christian community I ever could have asked for.

To all the people who feel alone, misunderstood, or unable to express what they're processing (and to all the women who've always wondered what's going on in guys' heads), thank you for taking the time to climb inside my mind and to walk with me on my broken journey.

Isaiah Stratton

NOTES

Chapter 5: New Year's
1. *The Book of Eli*, DVD, by Gary Whitta, directed by the Hughes brothers (Burbank: Warner Bros. Pictures, 2010).

Chapter 7: Summer
1. Denise Hildreth Jones, *Flying Solo* (Ventura, CA: Regal, 2010).

Made in the USA
Charleston, SC
03 May 2014